SO-CGS-143

THE
NOVICE
MOURNER

THE

Novice
Mourner

Joshua McKinney

Winner, 2005
The Dorothy Brunsman Poetry Prize

Bear Star Press

The Novice Mourner © 2005 by Joshua McKinney
All rights reserved
Printed in the USA

10 9 8 7 6 5 4 3 2 1

For permissions and information, please contact
BEAR STAR PRESS
185 Hollow Oak Drive, Cohasset, California 95973
530.891.0360 / *www.bearstarpress.com*

Cover: *The City of Omens* by Claudia Bernardi
Segura Publishing, Mesa, Arizona

Author photograph: Deni Polstra

Book design: Beth Spencer

The publisher wishes as always to thank Dorothy Brunsman
for her generous donation of the prize.

ISBN: 0-9719607-6-3
Library of Congress Control Number: 2005923038

Acknowledgements

I extend my gratitude to the editors of the journals and presses in which many of these poems appeared:

The Antioch Review: "Gun"
American Literary Review: "Reflective Property," "*Fort-Da*"
Boulevard: "Quick"
Chattahoochee Review: "A Rescue"
Cider Press Review: "The Secret"
Colorado Review: "Of What Use," "Happy," "In Extremity"
Cream City Review: "Unmaking the *Manes*"
The Distillery: "Falling Asleep by the Fire"
Fine Madness: "Nursing Home"
International Quarterly: "In Other Words"
The Kenyon Review: "In Earnest"
The Laurel Review: "Midden," "The Dark," "A Theory of
        Consequence"
New York Quarterly: "Chicken Slaughter"
Nevada County 2002 Anthology: "Alias," "Empire"
Pavement Saw: "Other Like Occasions"
Ploughshares: "A Principle of Perspective," "What We Wish For"
Phoebe: "Orphancy"
Santa Clara Review: "The Novice Mourner"
Sycamore Review: "Vigil"
Willow Springs: "Metaphysical"
Volt: "Trust"

"In Earnest" appeared in the Tebot Bach California Poets Anthology 2005, and also appeared on VerseDaily: www. versedaily.org. "'ve" and "Metaphysical" appeared in the chapbook *Permutations of the Gallery* (Pavement Saw Press 1996).

For my father,
Robert Floyd McKinney
1942-1984

Contents

Later he would remember all those dead voices
And call them Eurydice.

—Jack Spicer

This, then, was the complete game—disappearance
and return.

—Sigmund Freud

QUICK

To tell it correctly,
one must give
all the information at once.

A boy sits sick in a poem.
From a window he watches others
outside in snow.

Carving bone-white hills,
a few quick words
leap ahead of sleds.

Snow sifts into the corners
of the room,
heals his cluttered papers,

fleshes the bare branches
of trees, ruined by white
blossoms and leaves.

Chicken Slaughter

A man with a hatchet and a son walks out
to the hoof-pocked center of his barnyard.
A chopping block squats between them,
a wash tub ready to catch blood. At six, the boy
begs for a part in this, happy to leave
the women plucking and boiling near the barn.
Here dead birds fight to fly and hornets drone
above piles of white heads. The man smiles, drunk
with love for his son who crawls
from the coop, a hen drowsy in his thin arms.
He brings birds, pauses between trips to study
the work: the grip on the wings, the quick
snap of his father's wrist. Even in the interval
before the hatchet falls, the boy hopes
to learn, watches rubies bead from the blood-
wet wood, tries to decipher each scar in the block.
Behind a long shadow he comes clutching
the last bird, eager as his father motions him
forward to a bloom of neck feathers, an old hen
squinting against a low sun. And as the head
pops off and life leaps and leaps from the body,
the man stands helpless as the frightened boy
struggles, the headless bird so suddenly
alive in his hands.

HAPPY

The boy looks up from his army men
on the floor before the couch he is happy.

Used toys beat up scored with teethmarks
from some other kid but his now.

Above him his parents sit his father reading
always reading his mother mending

another kid's shirt but his now.
Come Monday he will wear it to school.

His mother smiles looks at his father
the needle glides mid-stitch

through air hovers an inch above
his father's thigh. The boy watches

his father reading his mother smiling
the needle moves closer his mother's hand

his father's thigh the needle's point gone
somewhere through his blue jeans.

The boy's mother watches
his father's face reading.

The boy watches the woman's hand
her fingers pinch the needle goes deeper.

Then the man looks up slow
from the book slow. The boy cannot

move he hopes the man will not be
mad he hasn't flinched or spoken.

Then the man looks at the woman
hard the man says *are you happy*

now the woman looks to her hand
her fingers white holding

the needle she pulls it out *oh sweetheart*
she says *you didn't move I thought*

you didn't feel nothing she says
she is crying now *I thought you was*

MIDDEN

I unprepare for this waking as a dog.
Chicken feathers in my mouth, I take a last
ride snug near a jack in the trunk of a car.
In dreams I didn't have, one flock of many
gulls always rose above raucous mountains.
We were fascinated by tubes of life
in those years when we came out of our graves
daily with comic books and rifles. What
can I submit to balance the beauty of burning
tires, the broken back of a recliner?
Smoke is the world's lid. I remember this,
raking each morning from a grate like coals
of tradition. Double-handfuls of dark keep
nothing afloat in the hole where each word
comes from, and the trajectory of hope
is a lead bee whining free of a bowling ball's
gravity, faint, fainter. Timmy Swanson climbs
into a refrigerator and does not die;
I have drilled through the locks.
We grin at a mannequin's tits, me with my
dog-day smile. The car rocks through gravel
like a ship, my nose wet. Out there are the gulls
and the place where we once found candy.

A hole dug is a hole filled.
Disappearing into the deep nostalgia
beyond the cyclone fence,
sounds shudder and rush together,
harden time into perplexing,
uninhabitable regions. This is how
we remember it, heating up tires or air,
a facsimile of events held together
by Grandma's whatnots. X is said
to be conserved. Memories of excitement seem
to promise something, and these rooms
under the vaulted syntax of sculpture, armless,
sight falling heavy from their eyes,
scrutinize the verity of blanks.

Those exhausted know astonishment.
Wandering through Europe remains
so very like footsteps rhyming through marbled
corridors: Museum. Mausoleum. Flightless
birds disturb no bread crumbs.
When I was a boy, my toy box contained
alphabet blocks, their shaky edifice of fictions,
Babel exploding in a burlesque of fullness.
Each block, in turn, contained a measure
of its present state, my small fists free
of origins. They tell me my first word was *father*.
I tear it up, coax the bloated magpies
which refuse the littlest piece.
Such a situation is said to be stable.

And I remember my confinement
for refusing asparagus, the way my fingers
cramped beautifully under the pressure
of *NO* scrawled in crayon across

the patterned wallpaper. Even if true
such closeted needs will not allow
new vistas. A frame is not a window.
Anachronisms protrude from every angle
in this infinite museum whose borders
are everywhere. They tell me I am free
to leave, but the doors marked EXIT
are apparently made for children,
always smallest where *I* must enter.

DARK SOUNDS

The first fear is to be
sundered, separate from oneself
so newly naked and aware

of the body's barest symptoms.
Here is a boy barely
breathing; under covers the closer

dark shuts out the sounds a bit, but
the others his parents
have become still threaten

to deafen him with fact. What mother
or father first gave breath to
the night? Whose fucking first

shattered childhood's sweet
and unconditional dreams with
the horror of our sexual selves?

Huddled in his cave of quilts
he hears the howl of throaty
vowels like an affirmation of

some tortured and joyous labor
back to birth. And worse,
he feels not hidden half enough,

not even from himself.

GRACE

And when at last the summer sun
    had darkened the green fruit
        to a bruise-like hue,

and the plums hung heavy
    from the highest boughs,
        the child I was then dared

to shinny up the trunk,
    crotch and belly to the bark,
        to gain the first smooth fork,

and thence with spindly limbs
    to pull myself aloft.
        And still the best fruit,

out of reach, hung gemlike
    in the cloud-flecked sky.
        The crows began to lift then,

scolding my nearness to their world,
    and their wings unfolding
        sent a tremor through the tree.

Emboldened, I climbed on,
    yet so intent on hand and foot
        that my ascending head pressed up

into a hive I had not seen.
    And in confusion I descended then,
        all caution gone, half falling, half

flung to earth where I hit hard
    yet rose and stumbled on,
        a venomed halo round my head.

Uncertain what it was that caused
    my pain, I howled as much
        at ignorance, as I passed

beneath the orchard shade
    and up the path unto the house,
        my crawling scalp aflame.

My mother must have heard
    my cries, for she stood before the door,
        the morning news rolled in her fist,

and as I reached her fell to smite
    me on the head and neck, upon my
        burning back and arms, and even

on my swollen face, as the broken
    bodies of bees rained golden
        down onto my feet, as I writhed

under her terrible urgency,
    as I begged forgiveness
        for I knew not what.

Alias

I would rather have some living thing than all the treasures of the world.
        –from "Rumpelstiltskin," *Grimm's Fairy Tales*

How many tales begin that way,
as a yarn spun out of nothing,
which is to say, out of the vulgar
world of words? To steal in, and out
again, and then to lay claim
to truth, where light filters through
some thin reality, a refuge for a fantasy
dispelled. The problem is consensus.

If a miller's daughter is said to possess
a remarkable skill, we are desperate
to believe in it, as we boys believed
the summer we sauntered beyond our parents'
fears and entered The Heights. Of course,
we were discovered—in some old woman's yard,
lazy, spitting pits from the high branches
of her cherry tree. And when she demanded

our names, we were suddenly other,
straight-faced, delivering identities
no tongue could trace—spontaneous
creations, hybrids utterly without class.
Shameless, we marched past her,
through the garden gate, down shaded
streets to our own neighborhood, where
we laughed and became ourselves again.

How many tales end that way,
with the humble acceptance of self?
Isn't it about change, the poor
girl become a queen, transformed
by a little man with a name so strange

no ledger contained it? Yet the larger
bargain remains—arbitrary, if you
consider thinking makes it so.

From his hut in the forest he came for
his due: the promise of a living thing.
And when a mother told him who he was,
he believed her. He had become himself,
no other. Hence, in his rage, he tore himself
asunder. This is how we claim the tragic.
Despite his magic, he could not escape
the presumptive nature of his name.

WHAT WE WISH FOR

The boy could sometimes see, could sense
    his father's fondness for a thing.
        One Christmas he spurned comic books,
penciled "shotgun" on his list to prove
    he'd moved beyond the tin cans
        and the .22. En route to the rite of deer,
perhaps hunt birds . . . like tiny planes;
    safe in a blind, he'd take his time
        and zero in, and thus, he thought, he could
acquire the skill to bring a winged thing down.

What kind of birds he was not sure,
    nor could he have named his feelings
        as he crept downstairs at 5:00 a.m. to find
his gift unwrapped beneath the tree:
    a Winchester 12-gauge single shot,
        feather-light and purchased from a man
his father knew, a man with debts and mouths
    to feed, a man who'd said he needed cash.
        One man's desperation can become another's
gain, can lead a boy to standing
    with a shotgun and a box of shells,
        the desert his firing range, his pigeon
an old pie tin his father has tossed.

And as it spun into the late sun's glare,
    the boy took aim and saw it hover there
        in silhouette, like those photos in his sci-fi mags,
those saucers that he prayed were real.
    What he knew next was disbelief, as though
        he had recoiled from dream. His shoulder numb,
the hoax dawned in the dirt where he'd hit hard,
    his father looking dismally down,
        commanding him to rise and try again.

But when he forced himself to shoot
      a second time, teeth clenched and eyes closed,
           there was a click but no kick came.
By what volition he could not say, yet
      to the boy the silence seemed transgression
           of some natural law, of expectations overthrown—
for even in his father's hands the gun refused to fire.

They walked back to the truck at dusk,
      the boy somehow relieved, determined
           not to try again, his father, hurling curses
at the sky, then saying with resolve, as if
      a promise to himself, that he would get his
           money back, by god, he would.

A Principle of Perspective

Call it the distance at which certain universals quiver into focus. Call it a kind of motif in the face, a relief in recognition, a cathartic thrill from the comfort of a couch. It's why a Russian can write of slow death, and an American can feel his scrotum tighten as he reads the tale—even in translation—then walk away refreshed. And it allows an Englishman to write of love and loss, and for a boy in Iowa to read those words and feel he knows that courtier's life though of his own he don't know shit—verily, not even the teat in his hand that fills the foaming bucket up. He's far too close, and that's the point. But add perspective and it comes:

It's a clear morning and the chores are underway. In the feed lot some border has been crossed, and a son stands face to face with his father—at the distance no human voice can bridge, the distance at which lovers whisper promises. Something in their stance is wrong, too still, too tense. It's hard to read precisely what it is that sends his mother running from the hen house, her apron full of eggs. She has seen it come to this before, the son knocked down by the father who stands there as the boy learns how to crawl again. But today it is the son who stands. He has broken the vessel of his father's face and released the secret hidden there behind the hate, that grim slate on which he tallies up his losses to the world. On hands and knees in hoof-scarred dirt, the father searches for the breath driven from his lungs by a punch the son has telegraphed for years—each time his welling words were bitten back, each time he had to pay for something that he did or didn't do. Perhaps in time he will construe the way the Herefords waited patiently, expecting hay that he would never give again, how he heard his mother's pleading cry, of the relationship of subjects to each other, to a whole.

The son has climbed the fence and strides now, quickly down the road. His back is turned; he will not see the farm again except in dream. The old man sees him go as he has seen it coming: the day hell would freeze over his dead body. There is an irony that withers there because the son has gone and cannot see the old man shaking off his wife, who hovers near to help him as he struggles to his feet and wipes a sleeve across his bloody mouth. Perspective requires a distance they do not possess, but we who watch them from the vantage point that words provide can see each face and place them side by side. Both father and son refuse to register shame or the pain in bloody face or hand, though surely these are buried there. What is the countenance they share? It is not pain; the cast is far too sinister, as though some darker double stood behind the bones. Or the ghost of a twin drowned for its failings. These faces, old and young, are one—honed down to nearly nothing by willful subtraction. No, the look lodged there is not like shame, nor even pain, but something like pain's closest kin—I see it now—a kind of satisfaction.

ORPHANCY

I abandon a bowl of fruit
to the shadow-mouth
the little gate off its hinges
I will never tell
what I saw in the attic
the sleeves
of this too-large coat
wave in an erratic wind carries
scraps of talk-
troubled firemen
the lane predictably soggy
as I take off my bronze
boots the country girls
smile from wagons
tossing ribbons and apples

THE NOVICE MOURNER

This may not be the end of something.
If the cat in the window knows anything,
she's not talking. For three days

his hands have smelled of pine,
clear eyes closed to study the blue moon
where the hammer kissed his thumb.

Food shadows lengthen, counting lulls
between determined moans of ambulance
and cottonwood. All those dishes to return.

His neighbor leans on a lawnmower
purple-faced; even his once luscious
wife wears life like a thin gown.

He scans obituaries for names of the living.
The mail slot sings its avalanche of grief,
anticipating spaces for every shotgunned

sign post, for every forgotten squash
turning to water under a canopy of leaves.
Any minute now, the phone rings.

GUN

SNAPPER

The boy and his father have come to the Nishnabotna bottoms because no one owns it and they can walk there because no one owns it. They park the pickup near the bridge and step out, then see a snapping turtle in the road. Its shell is cracked. It moves its legs but cannot move. The boy observes that people should watch where they are going they should not run over animals. The father looks down the road that narrows to nothing on its way toward town. He draws his pistol from the holster at his hip, aims and fires a single shot through the turtle's head. He lifts it by a hind leg and carries it off the road.

BONNIE PARKER

In the photo the boy's mother poses in front of a red 1957 Thunderbird, left foot in a black high-heeled pump propped on the chrome bumper. She is wearing black fishnet stockings and a short skirt. A white blouse open at the throat. She is young. Her long hair shines in the sun. Her right hand holds a pistol, its barrel trailing groundward along her thigh.

PUT DOWN

Greyhound/Irish Wolfhound cross, his name is Buck. He has been with the family since before the boy was born. He is the father's dog. There is a photo in the family album of the boy, small, sitting astride the dog. Now the dog is old, his kidneys shot, a foxtail so deep in his ear the vet cannot retrieve it. His head is swollen; the abscess leaks pus into a wool army blanket in the gravel-floored garage. One day he can barely rise to piss and the father sits at evening and cradles the stinking head, strokes a rib-strewn flank. The next morning a pistol's report wakes the boy. He lies listening for his mistake, stares up from his bed at the Zeros and Messerschmidts suspended from the ceiling by fishing line. Then the screen slaps shut and the back door and then more doors and even so from his parents' bedroom he can hear the terrible sound of his father weeping.

A LESSON

The boy's father shows him how to load and unload the gun, how to take it apart. He tells him its name: a Ruger "Blackhawk" .22-caliber single-action revolver. His father shows him how the thumb must be firm on the hammer how if it slips the gun will fire how because of this the gun should be pointed at the ground and away from people to never point a gun at a person. The boy's father tells him that if he follows these rules and the gun goes off no one will be hurt. He shows the boy a hole in the living room floor where his mother's thumb slipped when he was teaching her because she was afraid. You must not be afraid, you must hold the hammer firmly, if you are not afraid nothing will happen. Then the boy's father shows him how to clean the Ruger "Blackhawk" .22-caliber single-action revolver.

QUICK

The boy's father takes long walks alone in the desert. The boy's father takes long walks alone in the mountains. One day the boy's father is walking alone practicing his quick draw when his thumb slips off the hammer and the gun goes off mid-draw. The bullet hits a rivet in the holster and shatters. One tiny piece of shrapnel travels through blue denim and into the flesh of his thigh, the rest of the bullet drives into the dirt an inch from his foot. The thigh wound heals over the piece of lead inside. The father does not know it is there. A month later he will come to understand. He will make his wife extract the shard with a kitchen knife.

No Hard Feelings

The boy's family is driving to the mountains where they will walk. They must turn toward the lake. There is a truck in the distance there is time to make the turn but the truck is upon them pulling a boat on a trailer. Its brakes lock the tires make noise and black marks in the road. Both vehicles pull over. Two men approach his father's side of the car. He rolls his window down a crack. You son of a bitch, one man says, you damn near got us killed. There was time, the father says, you were driving too fast. Get out of that car you son of a bitch, the man says. You're the son of a bitch, the boy's mother says, I can smell the booze on you from here. Get out of the car, the man says. I don't want to get out, the boy's father says. Get out or I'll drag your ass out, the man says. The boy's father opens the door and steps out. The pistol is in its holster at his hip and he unsnaps the thong that holds the gun secure. The men's eyes travel to the Ruger "Blackhawk" .22-caliber single-action revolver and up and down the father facing them. We're heading to the lake for a barbecue, the man says, we had a few beers and maybe I was going too fast no hard feelings.

Family Outing

The boy and his parents take target practice at the dump of a weekend. It is a good place to shoot lots of things and no cleaning up. It is the dump you can break glass and leave it it is the dump. Today they have the rifles too and he is getting good not as good as his father but good. He hits his target every time. One time he found a dead dog someone had shot and his father cursed and cursed that someone would do that. One time he found some candy Rainbow Vendors threw away but he didn't eat any. One time he found a *Penthouse* and shot the pin-up through the tit. His mother is a good shot too she likes the pistol more her size she says she likes the way it kicks a little not too much. They pause to reload. He wades out looking for more things to shoot and the gulls lift up up and away.

HOME FROM SCHOOL

The bus brakes sigh and the door springs open to expel the boy who steps down onto the road's soft shoulder. Books slung at his back he crosses the creek and walks up the dusty lane beneath the pines. Near the house he hears the whine of the vacuum cleaner. He lifts a flowerpot from the porch rail, finds the key, unlocks the door. Through the kitchen the smell of fresh-baked bread, wood stove still hot. His mother is vacuuming the living room rug, the pistol in its holster at her hip. Careful to be loud he says he's home. Oh hi honey, his mother says, vacuuming.

SHOPPING

The boy and his father have been for a walk in the desert. The boy found an arrowhead with a broken point and he is happy. The boy thinks his father seems happy, so he asks if they can buy some ice cream. His father looks at him. They stop at the Eagle Thrifty and his father wears the pistol into the store. The boy follows his father down the aisles toward the frozen food. As they walk the other shoppers' eyes follow his father, dart to the Ruger "Blackhawk" .22-caliber single-action revolver and away. His father looks straight ahead, seems to hear and not hear the whispers. Get the kind you want, his father says, and the boy picks chocolate because he knows his father likes it.

HOME ALONE

One day the boy is home alone. He wonders. He takes the gun from beneath his parents' bed. He sits on their bed. He takes the gun out of its holster and carefully unloads it. He checks the cylinder twice to make sure it is empty. He counts the cartridges. He checks the cylinder again. He holds the gun in his right hand, cradles the barrel with his left. It is a pistol. It is a Ruger "Blackhawk" .22-caliber single-action revolver. Then he raises the gun and presses the barrel to his temple. He holds it there, cool where it touches the skin above his jaw. He is already afraid and he glances to the blanket where the six cartridges lie in a row. He wonders how some people can do it. He pulls back the hammer, can feel the metal slide on metal—one click, two clicks—the vibrations ripple down the barrel, the sound tall in his ear. He isn't depressed. He doesn't want to die. He feels ill and lowers the gun. Empty, he points it at the floor and eases the hammer down. If his father caught him he would be furious. He can feel his heart.

CALLED

The man's father has been dead twenty years. His mother has remarried. She lives far away and he doesn't see her much. Sometimes she calls. He has the gun. He bought a case for it. The gun is his now, but his wife does not like guns and he keeps it hidden. Once when they were dating he took her to the dump and showed her how to shoot it. She had never fired a gun. He let her hold it. He told her it was a Ruger "Blackhawk" .22-caliber single-action revolver. He showed her how to load it and how to ease the hammer down and how to aim and fire but she did not like it even then. He has not fired it in years. It sits high on a shelf in a dark closet. His son knows nothing of the gun. Sometimes, maybe once a year, the man takes it down and cleans it though it stays clean in its case. He thinks his wife has forgotten it and he is careful not to speak of the Ruger "Blackhawk" .22-caliber single-action revolver. Sometimes his mother calls. If his wife answers she will say just a minute and she will hand him the phone with her look. He will talk to his mother. They talk about this and that. Sometimes she asks about the gun, does he still have it, does he ever shoot it though she knows he does not. He says he still has it of course he still has it. Then he asks about her husband, how is he, he says, her husband. Don't ever get rid of it she says.

FALLING ASLEEP BY THE FIRE

I am not arguing that recollected
sun is warm. The center
and circumference of memory opens
a small door
in the house's side
where my father lies down on ice.

I reach into the belly, imperiled,
lumped willy-nilly,
pausing halfway
for odious and irrelevant comparison:
his legs stuck out in snow
like stems,
the whole house settled on his chest.

I burn the house down
with enough self-reliance, a little jazz
stoked against genetics' bitter kingdoms.

My community, kerneled,
thaws in a fevered palm: waking up,
moments ago and too close
to the fire, I imagined him
moving under the floor,
the hiss of his blue-tongued torch.

The first concerns discomfort at finding
my father (a decade dead) in poems.

    As when, a few years back, I encountered him
    woodworking in the Catskills. It was late

his hands, *surer than his failing sight, caressed*
planed pine with knotty joints. In the end

    he stepped back, mopped his brow, considered
    the result: a coffin

or maybe a bookcase.
The tools were all in place.

* * * *

    Another time I'm fishing the Deschutes
    when just above my favorite riffle

he's teaching some kid to roll
cast. It was dawn and

    the river smoked with ghosts
    in the gray first light, etc.

* * * *

It goes on like this: hunting
deer in Michigan, dying on beaches, in jungles,

    playing chess in parks, beating
    some red-haired woman

as children hold their breath beneath a bed.
Last night I'm reading before sleep and

there he is, building the house I was born in.
"What's this?" I say, squeezing through the door.

"We never owned a house. You're no carpenter."
"Do you have a gun?" he says.

That's when I looked up from the page.
No doubt this will explain some things.

* * * *

The next occurs at noon on a crowded street
in a city where you're so lonely

the pigeons remind you of pigeons. Suddenly,
a man hurls himself against a wall so hard

his shadow, stunned, can't peel itself
from the surface. It's as if,

for a moment, his shape is painted there
among the names and insignias. It's in

that space, about the time it takes
to picture it, the onlookers vanish.

IN OTHER WORDS

Light tactics splay over the ground,
and the clothes twisting
in wind, the shirts and skirts
forming like tall thoughts,
make sight a plea for mediation.

What sinful, crazy architect
concocts a past in tatters?
The light. The wind. I grew up
tall, thinking the way a chain twists,
winching engines into air.

"Back in the spring of" is how
it begins. *In*, *at*, *on*—the little
words that make place possible.
Telephones revise the fields,
which is why I am twisting even now

into the patchwork of an old woman's
apron, her hands without tactics
to clothe her husband, naked,
stumbling into a field to call
his dog, dead now for years.

I call no one and the tale survives
another telling. We embroider place.
We clothe the wind and lash it
to our backs. Power is always naked.
How could I tell them his stories grew

better in his last months,
the squeamish garments of a past
cast away in tatters, his words
strangely light, attendant to the world
and free from the idea of it.

Nursing Home

Listen, you, and you,
walking down corridors edged by
nightmare cities coming down
brick by brick seeking a cure. I carry
his grandson, bomb with an uncertain fuse
past lolling heads ripe
fruit trembles in its socks.
Above the tent and a few
cheap elements the baby's hand presses
sticky to the glass
his buggly little-old-man's eyes
all from the same bag of marbles,
his veins the same weave
as his powder-blue cap.
Fugue in the blood, no,
not even that—in lymph which fools us
like water. On the way home,
bars of cloud float like fish over the freeway.
There is no object so foul
light will not make use of it.

THE SECRET

The limitless choices of the dispossessed
clutter the park. Benches, well-lit day-rooms,
and clean laughter from a past that, confess

it, was never less than full—all are dooms
that gather as small hymns against slowing.
Sooner or later, even the harsh tunes

of spring are played on utensils grown
blunt against tables and teeth. Grief appears
in the headlines and stays news. Just showing

your face is work enough. If anyone hears
a story, it sounds familiar. Take this one
for example: When I was eight years

old, my parents took me to a nursing home
to see my great aunt. I don't recall her name
or the reason we went or why I had to go.

What I remember is this: as I came
close, she caught me, pulled my face to hers.
She never said a word, but all the same,

she made me swear. That near, I saw the blur
in her eyes, smelled the sore on her cheek
that would not heal. And when she was sure

I knew, she let me go. I could not speak
it, the secret I came to understand
years later, the way the future leaks,

silent, certain, squeezing fissures in a dam
that breaks one day, a promise from the past,
to change at once the surface of the land.

The body's excess erodes its last
impulse toward silence. We can't conceal
the monotonous tunes, or that stare cast

across parks, across day-rooms where we deal
to death a solitary hand. We become
the secret we swore never to reveal.

In Extremity

the eyes wrung dry
and yet : just here :

    (beyond the glass)

these hummingbirds : aloof
they draw the sweetness from the blooms

    (beyond cafeteria walls)

a concrete quad in which we eat
spring sun between each watch

    (beyond those all in white)

who come and go

(they draw the fluid from her lungs)

    there is a point

we touch : and do not
near : and I approached : and hollowly I spoke
my truth :
    that in my garden I found a sharp-tailed snake
beneath a stone : a black stone : in my garden which is
my garden
that I do not own the snake:
Contia tenuis : which I named and held yet
could not hold   (my eyes :

the world had drawn them dry)
this lame : this useless : I am made to love
the crawling and the wingèd

their furious hearts : their throats aflame :
her black toes

VIGIL

In these last moments
    before dawn, when
        the silence in the house

is like the nothing
    that follows a slammed door,
        I take up my watch.

Across the street,
    a light is on in Swanson's
        place, where it has

burned all night, every
    night, since his wife died.
        He turns it off at 6:15.

Such observations kill
    time, as if here, hidden
        behind this pane of glass,

the self disappears, the past
    stilled as in premonition,
        as in labor over words.

Outside, the paper boy hurls
    the news at us, his bike a blur.
        Swanson comes stiffly out

of his house. I emerge from mine.
    We bend down, eager for word
        of elsewhere, and rising

again, we nod, as men do when
        there is nothing to say,
                when in that moment

before going back
        inside, we stare across
                the distance where

at first light,
        in spite of everything,
                the world takes shape between us.

III

A RESCUE

Remember the putrid sweetness
Of the formal garden? How
We gathered it along the curving
Afternoons, the light
Crisp as sheets which reeked
Of petals long after
We'd slept there—
I can recall it only now
That it clings untamed
To the eroded cliffs of memory.
Its rows collapse into stone
Scoured clean by big water that lifted
Our house (rented) on a morning
Five years into marriage,
The present falling backward
To distract us. I won't deny
The lies I told to anchor
Our bodies transparent on a bed
That spun downstream,
Its mirrored surface flailing
My thin wrists squared.
It was you who rescued us, finally,
Hurling everything forward
Until we lost sight of shore.
When I wrote down our story,
You burned it saying, "I remember you,
Stranger." You smile, silent
As the vessel crumbles, dissolves
In my listening grateful
You will never ask for another
Day as we are, that excess
Drowned, this emptiness
Something we saved.

METAPHYSICAL

Someone's life like that.

Virtuous moments
beaten to the thinness of light-
bulb glass.

When we were young,
your lips were a scarlet
thread. They are still.

Late by several happinesses,
our keen perception
sails about the house, all

measure and language like
a shattered vase glued again
with the conceit that binds us.

A Theory of Consequence

There is a theory that the material world
reasserts itself near the end. Hence, to learn
to pay attention is a virtue. Bored,
waiting for my interest to return,
I spent the afternoon aloft on the high-
tiered hay, watching a pair of barn owls stare
down from the rafters. Near dark, when the sky
seemed to descend and I was suddenly aware
of the frogs trilling in the irrigation ditch,
one bird rose, turned to stone, and flew away.
Then all was still. I could not say which
stayed behind, female or male. But one stayed.
Then I climbed down and passed beneath the one,
and knew fear and was glad again. Though you were gone.

THE PROBLEM OF REFERENCE

In the future, a moment from now, I'll be alone
with this past and its adamantine offenses.
Now, the only source of history, will have gone

on ahead into what was and be wholly done
in in the messy intersection of tenses.
In the future, a moment from now, I'll be alone

with the problem of reference, how one
hoards afterimages that create a crisis
now. Our only source of history has gone,

is going, going . . . and once again I can
not find us in that missing string of sentences,
the future. A moment from now, I'll be alone

with who we were and how I will become
someone else as I stare into this page that is
now my only source of history. I will have gone

silent, and my noise will be the obscene drone
of regret with its promises, its references
to some future moment. From now on, I'll be alone

in the midst of time, my new endings grown
monstrous, the anywheres of beginning just pretenses
to a future. A moment from now, I'll be alone.
Now, my only source of history, will have gone.

Unmaking the *Manes*

They refuse to teach destruction,
continuously the detail we long for
polishing stones, arranging smoke and blood
or plastic flowers in patterns handed
walking in our shadows
a trick we detect only as age opens
its empty hands to us. Memory
tightens in my chest, hugging a stone,
and there is no gun at my head. Only children
running up the path, my own
breath
          conspiracy of vapors my father
and his father and ones I know
only in their child-likeness, the way
they point guns or pikes or stones
angling against light as instruments
of measure exhaling a life's breath.
Who doesn't feel the terrible sickness,
smell a cure in new hair, in small
duplicate hands? It is no more
unimaginable than trees falling, a wave
from east to west, and our similar selves
can never accept sacrifice.
I have placed my child in a hollow
of the stone
               and for once they are silent.

TRUST

the skyward child shouts
in the center between toss and

fall the father's hands open
to receive and in receiving save

this trust adapts the skyward child
descending shouts into his father's

upturned face already his own
in prayer the first pristine

insistence that he will lift up his
hands not in anger that

there will be before him only
a son not the enemy himself

hovering still in the bliss of the toss
small zenith blocking the sun

before descent before his feet firm
on the ground of father to father to

father the shade in which he stands
afraid of some new form of love

the father's trust an upturned face
the heat of a hand against it

THE DARK

The fleshy veneer of books
and boyhood retreats
in the night-light's glow.
Every father knows that
when he rises,
rolling back the sheet and
stumbling down the hall,
the fear that goes before him is
his own. What if there is no one
in the bed, the imprint of
a small body merely, and no son?
Yet that absence is gone
as soon as the child begs comfort,
and he, the bringer of all good
things, dispels with words
what was not there
and slakes the thirst and lies
back down to sleep.
And then, assured once more
that one will mourn him
when he dies, he sighs,
closes his eyes, and asks,
for the sake of one beside him
in the dark, "Are you awake?"

FORT-DA

A father holds his hands before his face
and asks where he has gone. His daughter
laughs, feigns puzzlement, as if no trace
of him remains. This game will teach her
to conceal her disappointment on that day
when his palms will part, as if from prayer,
and nothing is revealed. No thing can stay
this transformation; she cannot lie there
wrapped in bunting near the hearth, and he
cannot stop hunting for the words that summon
to common membership yet remain free.
Volition is consumed by repetition:
Actaeon steps into the sacred grove again
and loses speech. Such is the punishment
beauty inflicts. Each wondrous word for pain
is spent, and thus we learn by accident
the tendency of sound to disappear.
The mind masters sense; the child forgets
the feel of rhyme arrested in the ear,
while the father remembers and regrets
his inability to stop the years
that will return to tear from him his hold
on youth. It is in her laughter that he hears
his own voice crying from a lesser world.

THE WAR AT HOME

It's Tuesday, nearly Christmas,
and the kids have gone to school.
It's the day I work at home, the day
we've planned to set aside
some time, a few hours, to talk,
to touch, to take a walk around the block
among the falling leaves, and then
beneath the quilts to feel the chill
go out of us. Perhaps to say
some soft and secret thing unplanned,
perhaps to doze—if only to wake
still holding one another—and then
to rise again, to carry the glow
of union through the day.

We sit down to read the news
and by the second cup of coffee,
stop. The specters of the daily dead
assert themselves, and I can read
the disappointment in her face,
and worse, the shadow of a tired resolve
that looms up now, a merciful distraction:
there are goods to buy, and the car needs
gas. And I, too, in the mood now
only to be intimate with my anger at
the world. What used to come so easily
to us is now the victim of our broader view,
which narrows like this season
and its sun, like our grim smiles
as we tell each other, silently,
that we will make no time for love.

REFLECTIVE PROPERTY

The desire that it be not otherwise,
unchanged and exactly as it is,
the gestures mediate, attention drawn

to the empty hand that remains empty.
I have driven for days and nights
to stand at the edge of a field.

Having come this far, it does not matter
who owns the land or what version
I will render. My people are gone,

and winter arrives from the factory
where a pin-up's analogue for beauty
reflects the dim light of day labor.

These furrows and seed-graves are
no different. The cycle saw the people
planted, and when they grew

no wind dispersed them. When movement
came, it came in the linear spasms of
grief. History was a dull weight

the color of bread. Its axiom turned
their eyes to mirrors. They had too little
of something. They alone possessed it.

Who owns the house at the field's edge?
In the yard a child sees me and runs
inside. A tire swings from a tree.

In another version no footsteps echo.
Some small Orpheus flees the stones
that follow him. If he escapes,

there is no wall to pin hopes on.
It is a rendering which turns the eyes
to stone so that each glance shatters

the world's self-evidence. Looking back,
hands fill with stone. Looking back,
there is a house and there is a row

of houses. Everything is intermediary,
a mindless pleasure or violence. Inside
this field, the tiniest orchestra winds

a version, which drops as a crow
toward some glitter on the ground. Looking back,
I own this land and it recedes.

Altered House

What the body knows is its convenience,
and the abolished is betrayal of its house.

In my brain's bare tree,
my dead cat clambers.

Within this house, the walls of my small city fall.
Within this house, the walls of my small city harden.

For she was docile and could teach.
For she cannot creep.

Lounge-reading, I reach to touch
where her warm weight was.

Animal annexed to my body,
jet where my palm struck sparks,

sleepy piece of electricity
so impossibly gone now

her lost body remains—
demanding phantom of my convenience.

In Earnest

Fall's gold is gone. The American
will reek another week or two
before the circling birds stop

dropping black along the river's edge
to feed upon the rotting fish.
One marks this season by the stench

of Kings—some picked to bones,
some bloated in the watery sun,
some carried home by fishermen.

A couple's Lab has slipped its leash;
it runs and will not be called back
until it rolls in what remains, to mask

its scent in throes of primal joy.
A pack of boys casts stones at one
that offers now as evidence

its last thrashing in the shallows
near the shore. I leave my footprints
with the rest. Along this edge

death is success; and its resolve to live
nowhere in earnest, now here in every
phase, is almost nothing, almost all.

OF WHAT USE

is it now
the clean constructions move
vanish at the boundaries?

Possibilities flare and darken .
the day altered
again . in one direction :
            the sea . in
            the other : the forest
farther than remembered .

I look up . having lost
an eye in the space of
a day the raccoon arrives
to eat the meat
the cat left .

EMPIRE

Blossoms and leaves can't stanch the light
that left the straightened gardens bent. Nor can sight
unhinge itself from the dark stain spread beneath
the trees. What's ample now is long in the teeth
soon enough the classics say. They name death night

and tuck it in. The bare limbs break; a man turns right
at a fork in the road. He meets his father and fights
to pass into the city—as if his keenest eyes bequeath
blossoms and leaves

to a familiar world. We know the tale, the blight
that lay like frost upon the land. And it might
be enough for us, if this irony, belief,
were brilliant fruit instead of bread, if grief
were not a mighty empire, which at its height
blossoms and leaves.

NOTES

"'VE" : Some of the language in this poem was taken, with gratitude, from Robert Smithson's essay, "Some Void Thoughts on Museums."

"ALIAS" is informed by, and infused with, the language and ideas presented in Donald Revell's autobiographical essay, "The Moving Sidewalk."

"UNMAKING THE *MANES*" : *Manes* 1: the deified spirits of the ancient Roman dead honored with graveside sacrifices. 2: the venerated or appeased spirit of a dead person.

"*FORT-DA*" : The term "*Fort-Da*" has its origin in Freud's case study of a boy who liked to hide his toys, then rediscover them. After putting them out of sight he uttered a sound like "fort" (gone); when he brought them back into view he exclaimed "da" (there). *This, then, was the complete game—disappearance and return.*

About the Author

Joshua McKinney was born on an Iowa farm and raised in the mountains and high desert of northern California, where he worked seasonally as a wildland fire fighter for the United States Forest Service. He holds a B.A. and M.A. from Humboldt State University and a Ph.D. from the University of Denver. In 1988 he travelled to Japan to study kendo, and he continues to be an avid practitioner of Japanese sword arts. His first book, *Saunter* (2002), was selected in the University of Georgia Press Poetry Series Open Competition, and he is also the author of two poetry chapbooks. He is currently an associate professor of English at California State University, Sacramento. He lives in Fair Oaks with his wife and two children.